Swaranjali

MOHAN

Become Shakespeare
.com

First published in 2020 by
BecomeShakespeare.com

One Point Six Technologies Pvt Ltd.
119-123, 1st Floor, Building J2, B - Wing,
Wadala Truck Terminal,
Wadala East, Mumbai, Maharashtra, India, 400022.
T:+91 8587995915

ISBN: 978-93-90266-02-9

DEDICATED TO

To my mother and my nation

ACKNOWLEDGEMENTS

The idea of writing a book of poems would not have been possible for me but for the generosity and goodwill of a variety of people, includinga myriad social interactions I had in my day to day life.

In writing this heartfelt book, I am deeply indebted to my parents, siblings and friends for their unflinching and unconditional love. I am ever grateful to my teachers who have taught me the values of life.

Special gratitude to all my friends who have always encouraged me to explore the craft of writing.

I, sincerely, thank the publishers at become Shakespeare for their patience and enthusiasm in guiding me through the different stages of publishing. My heartfelt thanks to Pooja, Pranali and Shreyas for their unrelenting support and guidance throughout.

CONTENTS

MY DEAR FRIEND

Peeping in through the windows of my curiosity, I delve into the river of thoughts flashing through my brain endlessly..

I am recommended to open my doors of perception to you my friend, Guide me into the light of wisdom that illuminates the life of the perturbed soul..

It is into you my friend, I confide and feel the warmth of trust,comfort and unattainable easiness..

Never throw me into the hands of a chaotic and ruthless world , that's amiably hateful, jealous and miserable..I Scream!!!

SUNDAY RAIN

As the Sky gets ready to shower the earth, the birds come out of their homes to dance and rejoice in the fauna-wood

It's another flight that has taken off against the winds…

The clouds roar heavy and have no mercy

as the pearls scatter on the soil adding to its beauty.

The rhythm of the waterfall is only a sign

to remind us, the love of nature is in no hurry to resign

With the strings of heart playing the symphony,

The world is at peace with the endangered animosity

The trumpet is blown in the sky, only to signal it's time to fly.

THE NEGLECTED

Seeing the empty bodies on the street without hearts and minds,

The inside screams hey! dude open your eyes and stop pretending

It's a constant sorrow to watch consciences being raped by human desires

The characters assassinated by human greed, and the wheel of life rides on

The humanity is in shambles as every tear of poverty is wearing away the rock

the weather is damp, cold, wet and dark

The light seems a distant dream and the life crawling about on the earth..

Gods of prosperity have been on a holiday

seems to 'em no urgent matter if the world is grey

ships are in shaky waters, shipping along,

And the moon fighting its way out of the clouds.

INTELLIGENTLY FOOLISH - DARLING! HEART

After a long sombre sleep, You wake up only to realize that forcing things to shape up the way your expectation leads you to is like trying to catch your shadow in the dark,

Though the heart prefers to be fooled as much as it could be inside the cloth of fancied dreams, more often than not it ends up being the victim of someone's ignorance and pretence.

And how much significant that Someone is to the heart, can be read by the scars shining on it, as the Foolish heart condones that someone while chasing its fancied dreams.

But let that someone know that my time and my thoughts can no longer be held hostage to his/her tailored and creative ignorance,

Teaching the foolish heart the nuances of practicality and logic is not very easy, but the train of wisdom is never too late to catch.. I am boarding!

NOMADIC NO-MAD

Walking down the uncertain alley, with the thoughts vibrating in my mind..

I offer paeans of life's constant effort to recourse against the capricious winds

The nomad from the tribe is on the ship sailing and sailing,

realizing the journey being longer than his age.

NAKED EXPRESSIONS IN DISGUISE

Open the doors!

you see those faces caged in the balconies of their apartments

eyes talking to each other, asking if we could hangout?

The sun's burnt enough, time it flames down steadily.

the sports are over and the kids on the streets screaming to the sky!

i better run to the moon now to sit in its lap and listen to the legends about the stars….

Another beautiful day in this paradise sleeps..really?

PRAYER IN VACUUM

Oh! Lord, Thou know my dreams, honor thy patience.

amidst the raging clangours of these dreams, acts are curfewed.

Liberty of desired imagination is massacred by the baggage of mistakes from the past.

This head bows in the court of time before thou.

Strength, patience & life to these dreams of my fellow men..

In these strange times, with the continuity of life's seeming a riddle,

Solution lies in thy love, blessings and direction, as We curiously roam in the fair.

VOLCANIC EMOTION

Lying on the sand in the agonized desert I am tired and broken. I don't want to walk no more in the false belief of finding an oasis called Life. I capitulate myself to the shackles of Lord's theatrical play.

My life is not mine anymore. I give up chasing it as I see it as a futile attempt. Life has been a hard master, but today I refuse to learn lessons from it as my strength to learn and tolerate this loss is negligible.

If suffering had to be my destiny, then I let fate have the last laugh on the cruel joke played. I seek no peace..no more. The pain is hard to explain as the words fall short of the near vague description.

As I stand exposed to the vulnerabilities of the material world, I lack the skill of trading emotion for logic, pain for reasoning and sorrow for intelligence.

Oh! Lord, few of your men have looted the jewel of my life.

MARCH ON!

In the soil, is the past,

In the skies, is the future

my aspirations breathe in

the presents' galore.

Living the Love until i live

endowing the couthy memories, for the history to weave..

Hang on, as we begin the journey one more time,

holding onto the silly pockets without a dime.

HANGING DREAMS

Imprisoned in the walls of ignorance

my mind provokingly beams

I got a Dream, I got a Dream

to swim with the kites in air, to race with the clouds

to sleep on the moon, to hug the stars

trapped in the cobweb of material hunting

my soul annoyingly screams

I got a Dream, I got a Dream

to sing to the world from the mountains of Everest

to dance with the men/women of thou tribe, O' Lord

I got a Dream. I,indeed, got a Dream.

SON, UP YOU GO NEXT!

From the hungry lion's prowl to the screeches of the owl,

The ring is all decorated for the infamous brawl.

The winner is rewarded a chance to fight one more day

& the loser dies, as he disappears fast in the pitch-dark bay..

With the obvious sense of fear, the audience collates to crowd the winner

Fights on every night, deaths replaced by lives and lives by deaths.

Swiftly the winds come yelling – "you are up next"..

and I am,little hesitatingly, thrown out to fight one more day.

FACELESS GYPSY

I exchanged the looks of promise and hope with the her,

tenderly the shoulders dropped and gently the handshake fell, her eyes demanded explanation.

My eyes were speechless as I cowardly looked down to earth searching for words

But the body had to answer the call of duty,

Mind prevailed over heart so swiftly

In the midst of broken memories branching out of those good times

the faceless gypsy is unceasingly

trudging up the terrains and ploughing into the forests

in a constant trawl for treasure – PEACE!!

LULUS OF ACCESSION

Over the rim of desire, patience slips and thoughts die

pushed into the gutter, the intimacies of principles dry.

The cuckold griefs, as the whine is send

much to his dislike, the night doesn't end.

Reads the undelivered letter that he once wrote,

to the beauty, the smile it brought.

the flowers bloomed and the butterflies sang

the riverbed orchestrated the music, inhabiting it the fishes danced

chronicle of heartbreak is hard to comprehend

the false prevails one more time, following the conventional trend.

MERCHANTS OF WAR

You play this game with petty fame and absolute no shame.

you invent the toys, choose the boys and design the ploys.

you seek peace with wars, you trade blood for blood,

Oh! you merchants of war open your eyes and shut your mind

You come as someone, do not spare anyone, and then leave as a someone

Who told you, you conquered? bloody moron, you will burn in the sun

you say you conquer the lands, but who shall conquer your wailing soul,

Oh! you merchants of war open your eyes and shut your mind

Death never follows, it strikes

so what if you fly on your motor bikes

Drop the guns and tear the bombs,

could you, chase your soul, whistling in the woods?

You claim the prophets, you guard them, you become them, and you kill them!

Oh! you merchants of war open your eyes and shut your mind.

TIME OF UNION

At the cow-dust hour, it's a majestic union of the sun and the moon.

A beatific vision with the birds, the monkeys, the rats return to their places of residence.

The bliss of returning home after the worldly hunting,

The sound of the laughter of the sleepy little child

elicits the raptures of strayed soul,

slowly drowning in the deeps of the oceans of the world.

From which land you came?

to which sky you would fly?

the quest for the truth travels through the beads.

As water and waves are the same,

so do thoughts and actions

As I swept all tinsel away,

I have arrived at this Union.

SOMETIMES!

Sometimes!

Night is not the absence of light, it's the refusal of Sun to shine

Ignorance is not the absence of knowledge, it's the denial of known

Hate is not the absence of love, it's the resignation of love

Sometimes!

Chaos is not the absence of peace, it's the submission of peace

Lie is not the absence of truth, it's the silence of truth

Greed is not the absence of soul, it's the withdrawal of soul

Fear is not the absence of courage, it's the capitulation of courage

Sometimes!

INFINITY

YOU are the proof to my dreams i see in day & at night

the fragrance of your body hypnotizes my soul

YOU are the smile on my eyes, the music on my face

the breathe that travels through the landscape

of my body at an exhilarating pace

How do I quantify my love for you?

It begs neither an adjective, nor an adverb

My love is you, you are my love. Simply put.

How can my heart conquer yours?

Hearts are not at wars to win or lose

Hearts are the stars of one big constellation, shining for each other

when do we meet is the question for time to answer

Meanwhile, I whisper to my heart – When did you really leave?

DICTATING ENIGMA

Let us walk down the valley of dictating enigma

where still is the blind man,

who sees the world through his heart

while the shapes of human experiments

callously interfere with the order of nature

As he meditates and scouts for the meaning of self-existence

the world with its stubborn chase for life intimidates him to toe the line

Darkness is his light, concentration his lamp

His world of human settlement has no borders

His dreams are not bound by the frontiers of desire

Before the eyes, He desires a world he can see.

DECIPHERING SHADOWS

When the histories are progeny of prophecies

of saints, scriptures, sculptures and stones

When the glory is seemingly glorious in the doom

and the elephant is dancing in a sheep's room

When the traditions are blindfolded by the superstitions

and the guardians are the new custodians

When the Legends of yesterday are visions for tomorrow,

perhaps the country is in a cherished sorrow

When the body walks in the blazing sun light

No wonder! the shadows appear strikingly bright.

GHETTOS OF THE MUNDANE!

Decorated in his shorts and shoes, he painted his childhood

On the bicycles he rode,infamous trivial ambitions for the future got bored

As he entered the playground, the friendship was even more proud

then the boy went to the school, in hope to be in the brighter pool

sooner he realized: The grumpy marionette was in-charge of puppets and fool

Terrified he ran for his home

taking the same route he had taken before

while the winds were heavy and the dust stuck on his face, it distracted his speed

He was at the crossroads,

stopped and gazed at the theater

with seemingly homogeneous actors-audience

From a distance, the sight was enchanting in the exotic trans

ignoring any further hindrance or delay he runs into the theater, innocuously involved, switching his role between an audience and an actor

Slyly the time slips by,

Well! It's the ghettos of the mundane.

RISE AS IT STANDS

Morning has been voluntarily released

by the tired and ebbing night

the screaming cock crowing in its discovered might

gleaming sun rays,

piercing through the narrow passage between the window frames,

stumbling on the dead table and the reluctant pen,

enlivening the abandoned pages

new stories are to be written,

new shores are to be discovered,

rise as the morning stands yet again,

faiths are to be put on trial by the judicious destiny,

Laugh, hug, believe, Love – Good Morning!

FROM THE HINTERLAND

When,

the brain cells lie frozen,

the blood in the veins have dried,

the oxygen in the heart is polluted,

broken are the descending limbs,

then,

you appear my love,

a caravan of memories arrive,

out of the casual breeze of eternity,

fragrance of life strikes

The Silence speaks,

Stay! Don't go away, would you?

ALL THE WORLD'S A BIG BUS

Packed all my stained clothes in the ruck

In the backyard, buried all the muck

alluring birds take the flight

ungodly snakes the downfall

together held in repelling gravitas

the waving leaves and upon the discreet bloom

Oh dear! make no fuss!

time to rush! get on the bus!

THIEVES IN MOTION

Disbanded by its own memories,

Disowned by its own soul,

Disrobed by its own body,

Discharged of its own emotions,

Thieves & Thoughts

in motion everywhere

evading, diluting, screening through

the curtains of familiar hazy smoke.

SILENT MUTINY

As the wounded soldier takes guard behind the rocks

hoping the sun goes down and the clouds close in

descending shooting stars tantalize his sinking courage

Away from home,

he hugs the mother earth

kisses the homeland,

soaked in blood,

the glory keels over

A VERSE IN DRAFT

Hey! No, It's ain't finished yet

The tortuous winds have only just arrived

borrowing the wood from the silent nature

I redesign my armour to dive in the blue

Epic is a short word, Legendary would be too modest

It's the convergence of ages, fusion of the egos

No birth no death, evading it's record in time

Floating are the coins,

lighter than the oceans,

the heart is not heavy as yet

Come on! Here I stand! – uproot me!

STREETS OF STEEPING DESIRE

Woken up on the drowsy streets in a desolate land

broken were the ears by the sounds of a forgotten band

That piercing gaze from the pied piper, shaking down the lazy spirit

I am up on my feet, trembling and stumbling,

hitting another dead man who's falling

hypnotized by the pied piper, my eyes are blacked out

It's the streets of steeping desire

with its unrelenting lousy scheme to hire

Raining thoughts and drizzling optimism on fire

trudging up on the streets of steeping desire

Though everything seems hazy and grey

I am told, due promise is merry and gay

well! how can then my dragging feet tire?

trudging up on the streets of steeping desire.

DICHOTOMY

Under the blue umbrella, we shared the little joys

together we waved to the day sinking into the clouds

today when we are seas and worlds apart

all those memories refuse to depart

wheeling across the lanes, pushing the cart

little did we know, lying was then an art

time remained a constant and we the variable

skewed zigzag into the chain, woven into the bubble

Oh! we jumped higher, defying the gravity

Oh! we laughed harder, defying the space

In the midst of open muddy fields,

sizzling brown under the sun

exterminating the thorns from the blooming flowers

we sat, and together we prayed for the divine showers

The inertia of memories ply the unstoppable wheels of life

EFFERVESCENT PASSION

The glory shone bright

in the dreams from the last night

fallen is the will

refusing the morning drill

when the time's a moving

I stand here still

It's not too late, as the winds caution

diffusing is the effervescent passion

Yesterday, when the candle meddled with the darkness of the night

up came the breeze from the south that settled down the passing light

While i am closed in here, it feels so tight

not one to trace, nothing in sight

It's not too late, as the winds caution

diffusing is the effervescent passion.

FREEDOM APPARENTLY!

Continents, countries, cultures, communities, customs and couture

overlapping in the layers of over-sized ambitions

Slaying for supremacy and survival

Bleeding minds, Freedom apparently..

Faith and Truth are just the words

echoing from alien worlds

it's red that colors the desires

amid the raging fires

Wounded hands, Freedom apparently.

MEDITATION

Will this ever end?

Did it ever start?

Why do the clouds constantly pass

Why does the sun stay still

Why is the moon always hiding

Why do the stars appear in a crowd

Why do I survive,

Why do I get back,

Why am I stronger than before

Curiosity seeped in thoughts

Thoughts keeping up with emotions

Words nibble through the thoughts

Words travelling far and wide

Meandering, searching and seeking

To be with the Gods and the Creators

Perambulating with many a shapeless energies

Vacillating between cosmic forms of untold stories.

In a space where chaos is hailed as the order of the unnatural mace,

Loud shall be your arrival, thunderous shall be your exit!

Go on! Go Beyond! Do Come Back!

BY THE FIRESIDE

Finding love is an illusion, or a trap

a map of emotions, without a cap

constantly you chase or walk but never stop

While at every moment of twists and turns

It is revealed and interrogated, by an ever fat cop.

The little games you play my behind

I lose my words, I lose my mind

Don't get me there, Oh! no darling!

Sweet as it may seem, secrets all carving

You kill me once, you kill me twice

Without a price, you do it so nice

The drama ends as I find myself lying

Characters dying, the butterfly flying

You play the face, behind the mask

Skilfully holding upto the task

What is the truth, what is the false,

What is the real, what is the farce,

I go till the end, I run to the edge

While everything hangs so loosely by the wedge

What is so far, what is so near

What is so lost, what is so dear

I can show you my heart, but dare you see?

For the shining scars or the gloomy fantasy

Get up and leave, please! leave, for one last time

Not all get this call, not even for the first time

Never come back, never look behind

You shall have half my soul and an empty mind

Take my coat to keep you warm

In the winds of summer, in the rains of winter

I would live here and die here as all poets do,

sitting by the fireside, chanting by the sky, delving into the blue.